100 great

Cocktails

We are grateful to Dublin (ITC Hotels Maurya Sheraton
& Towers, New Delhi), for facilitating the photography.

ISBN: 81-7436-283-5

© Roli & Janssen BV 2003
Published in India by Roli Books
in arrangement with Roli & Janssen BV
M-75 Greater Kailash-II (Market)
New Delhi 110 048, India.
Phone: (011) 29212271, 29212782
Fax: (011) 29217185
Email: roli@vsnl.com
Website: rolibooks.com

Printed and bound at Singapore

100 great

Cocktails

Tim Bryan

Photographs
Amit Pasricha

Lustre Press
Roli Books

Contents

No single version explains the origin of the name cocktail. Be that as it may, cocktails have come a long way since they were first 'invented' in the days of Prohibition in America (1920-1933). Apparently, in order to get past the temperance advocates of the times, alcoholic drinks were often disguised with fruit juices to confuse suspicious noses. However, by the fifties, cocktails had become the fashionable drink of the upper classes all over Europe as well. Popularized in books and films thereafter, bartenders devised new combinations to attract customers and vied with each other to put their names as signatures to popular alcoholic combinations. Statisticians believe that over seventeen million variations can be made with the spirits of a well-stocked bar. Naturally, no living human being can have tasted them all: one claims to have tasted 273.

We offer a selection of 100 cocktails for the beginners and the connoisseurs. Aimed at the host who enjoys entertaining guests at home with innovative food and drink, the selection offered here may trigger off a few personal 'discoveries' as well. The joy of serving a well-made cocktail is matched only by the joy of creating it and the recipes in the book offer a wide selection. There are suggestions here on what to offer guests from pre-dinner to post-dinner, with tips on glassware.

A few words of advice: always taste the drink before you inflict it on your guests. Lemons, for instance, vary in tartness according to variety and season, so if your creation is too sour or too sweet, add something to adjust it. In a perfectly balanced drink, you should be able to taste all the ingredients but they must be blended so well that they are difficult to fathom.

A word of caution: don't be too ambitious when starting out. Try your creations on a select company of close friends until you get the hang of shaking *one* perfect cocktail. Finally, always remember that the proof of the drink is in the drinking and no amount of style will ever disguise a bad cocktail.

If you are not fortunate enough to have a permanent bar in your home, the best place to set up your bar is really the kitchen. You need work top space, electrical sockets, washing up facilities, storage for both your glassware, ingredients, and a place to keep your ice. Set your bottles at the back of the bar and your glasses in front of them. Your minerals and juices should be kept underneath preferably refrigerated. Keep your work-top clean and clear. A well-stocked bar should have the following:

Equipment

Blender, shaker, barspoon, measuring cup,
mixing glass, bottle and can opener,
lemon juice squeezer, straws, swizzle sticks, paring knife,
cocktail napkins, ice-crusher, strainer

Liqueurs

Amaretto, Benedictine, Cointreau, curaçao,
crème de cacao, crème de cassis, crème de menthe,
Galliano, Kahlua, maraschino

Aperitif and Wines

Campari, champagne, red and white wine, vermouth

Liquors

Whisky, rum, tequila, vodka, brandy, gin

Mixers

Ginger-ale, lemon juice, lime juice cordial,
orange juice, tomato juice

Flavourings

Angostura bitters, grenadine, Worcestershire sauce,
Tabasco, cinnamon stick, cloves, honey, salt,
black pepper, sugar, cream, nutmeg

Garnishes

Celery sticks, cherries, mint sprigs,
lemon and orange slices, olives,
pineapple slices, strawberries

The range of glassware available is enormous. There are special glasses for wines of a particular grape variety. Although the correct glass is important you should not be too pedantic about which glass to serve with which drink. The most important thing to consider when deciding which glass to use is size. Don't choose a glass which will only be half-filled by the drink you have just made. Alternatively, you should not waste that drink by choosing a glass which is too small. The shape of the glass is also important as it helps to retain the flavour of the drink. To enhance the flavour of the drink and to add a touch of panache the rim of glass is frosted for example, Bloody Mary or Margarita. To frost, dip the rim of the glass into a saucer of lemon juice and salt or as specified.

There are two basic categories of glass, those with stem and those without. These are the basic types of glass with the approximate capacities, which you need once you decide to make your home the rendezvous for your friends.

With a Stem

1. Cocktail Glass — 270 ml
2. Wine Goblet — 420 ml
3. Champagne Flute — 240 ml
4. Champagne Saucer — 150 ml
5. White Wine Glass — 300 ml
6. Brandy Snifter — 360 ml

Without a Stem

7. Old-fashioned Glass — 300 ml
8. Collins Glass — 420 ml
9. Highball Glass — 360 ml
10. Pilsner Glass — 600 ml

Blend Put the ingredients into a blender with crushed ice until the required consistency is achieved but remember to blend longer if you are making a frozen drink. Blending is usually required when using solid fruits, ice cream, coconut cream or if the consistency of sorbet is required.

Build Pour the ingredients directly into the glass with or without ice as required.

Dash A very small amount.

Float To pour on top of other liquids without disturbing them.

Frosting Moistening the glass rim, usually with a lemon, to allow an ingredient to stick to the rim.

Muddle To mix a drink or stir an ingredient into a drink.

On The Rocks Drinks served undiluted and with ice cubes.

Shake Pour the ingredients into a cocktail shaker with ice. Shake quite violently without rocking the drink. Shaking is usually required when at least one of the ingredients is opaque.

Splash A term used when approximately 30 ml of liquid is added to a drink.

Stir Half fill a bar mixing glass or jug with ice, pour in the required ingredients, stir until drink is cold enough then strain into the glass. Stirring is required when all of the ingredients are transparent.

Twist A small piece of citrus peel which is squeezed over the drink so that the smell of the fruit can be enjoyed whilst sipping the drink

Ingredients:

20 ml	Gin
20 ml	Lemon juice
20 ml	Sugar syrup
	Champagne

Garnish:

None

Glass:

Champagne flute

Method:

Shake all the ingredients together except champagne and strain into a champagne flute. Top up with champagne.

Bellini

Ingredients:

60 ml	Peach juice
120 ml	Champagne

Garnish:

A wedge of peach

Glass:

Champagne flute

Method:

Fill one-third of champagne flute with peach juice. Top up with champagne and stir gently. Serve garnished with a wedge of peach.

Ingredients:

1	Sugar cube
3-4 drops	Angostura bitters
20 ml	Brandy
	Champagne

Garnish:

Orange slice or twisted orange peel

Glass:

Champagne flute

Method:

Soak the sugar cube in angostura bitters and drop it into the glass. Add brandy and top up with champagne. Serve garnished with a slice of orange or twisted orange peel.

Ingredients:

40 ml	Apricot brandy
20 ml	Fresh orange juice
140 ml	Champagne

Garnish:

None

Glass:

Champagne flute

Method:

Shake the apricot brandy and orange juice and strain into a champagne flute. Top up with champagne.

Ingredients:

10 ml	Crème de cassis
	Dry white wine

Garnish:

A twist of orange peel

Glass:

White wine

Method:

Pour the crème de cassis into the glass. Top up with white wine. For a Kir Royal, substitute the wine glass for a champagne glass and white wine for champagne.

Ingredients:

60 ml	Fresh orange juice
120 ml	Champagne
20 ml	Orange curaçao

Garnish:

None

Glass:

Champagne flute

Method:

First pour the orange juice, then the champagne into a champagne flute. Float the curaçao on top.

Ingredients:

2	Fresh strawberries
a dash	Fraise liqueur or
	fraise syrup
	Champagne

Garnish:

Strawberry

Glass:

Champagne flute

Method:

Blend the first two ingredients and pour to fill $1/3$ of the glass. Top up with champagne; stirring gently. Serve garnished with a strawberry.

Fraise Royale

Ingredients

Chilled Guinness
Chilled Champagne
In equal proportions

Garnish:

None

Glass:

Champagne flute

Method:

Half fill the champagne flute with Guinness and top up with champagne.

Ingredients:

30 ml	Lemon juice
10 ml	Sugar syrup
60 ml	Apricot brandy
a dash	Angostura bitters
	Soda water

Garnish:

None

Glass:

Highball

Method:

Shake all the ingredients together except soda and strain into a highball glass. Add ice cubes and top up with soda.

Ingredients:

40 ml	Vodka
40 ml	Tequila
80 ml	Orange juice
a dash	Galliano

Garnish:

None

Glass:

Highball

Method:

Build the drink in an ice-filled highball glass.

Freddy Fudpucker

Ingredients:

50 ml   Vodka
200 ml   Tomato juice
Worcestershire sauce, salt, pepper, lemon juice, Tabasco, and celery salt to taste

Garnish:

A wedge of lemon or anything suitable. Rim glass with salt or celery salt.

Glass:

Old-fashioned or Highball

Method:

Pour the ingredients straight into an ice-filled glass. Serve garnished with a wedge of lemon or anything suitable.

Ingredients:

40 ml   Peach liqueur
40 ml   Vodka
80 ml   Orange juice

Garnish:

None

Glass:

Highball

Method:

Build the drink in an ice-filled highball glass.

Bloody Caesar & Family

Ingredients:

60 ml	Vodka
120 ml	Clamato juice
a dash	Lemon juice

Worcestershire sauce, celery salt,
Tabasco and pepper to taste

Garnish:

A celery stick

Glass:

Highball

Method:

Shake all the ingredients together and
strain into an ice-filled highball glass.
Serve garnished with a celery stick.

Buck's Fizz

Ingredients

100 ml	Orange juice
10 ml	Champagne

Garnish:

None

Glass :

Champagne flute

Method :

Pour the orange juice first in a
champagne flute and top up with
champagne.

Ingredients:

30 ml   Martini red

30 ml   Campari

Soda water to taste

Garnish:

A slice of lemon

Glass:

Old-fashioned

Method:

Fill the glass with ice and build the ingredients. Top up with soda to taste. Serve garnished with a slice of lemon.

Screwdriver

Ingredients:

60 ml   Vodka

120 ml   Fresh orange juice

Garnish:

A slice of orange

Glass:

Highball

Method:

Build the drink in an ice-filled highball glass. Serve garnished with a slice of orange.

Ingredients:

30 ml   Amaretto

30 ml   Campari

140 ml   Limca

Garnish:

None

Glass:

Wine goblet

Method:

Shake the amaretto and campari in a shaker and pour into a wine goblet. Top up with Limca.

Ingredients:

50 ml   White rum

10 ml   Maraschino

30 ml   Fresh lime juice

10 ml   Sugar syrup

Garnish:

A cocktail cherry

Glass:

Champagne flute

Method:

Blend all the ingredients on high speed with a large scoop of crushed ice. Pour unstrained into a champagne flute and garnish with a cocktail cherry. Serve with a wide-girthed straw.

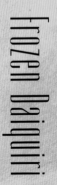

Ingredients:

10	Mint leaves, chopped
1 tbsp	Caster sugar
15 ml	Water
60 ml	Bourbon

Garnish:

None

Glass:

Highball or Old-fashioned

Method:

Grind the mint leaves and sugar with water until the sugar dissolves completely. Fill the glass with crushed ice; add bourbon and serve with a straw.

Mint Julep

Ingredients:

60 ml	Peach liqueur
120 ml	Orange juice

Garnish:

None

Glass:

Highball

Method:

Build the drink in an ice-filled highball glass.

Fuzzy Navel

Ingredients:

60 ml   Pimm's no.1

           Lemonade

Garnish:

Slices of orange, lemon and apple;
rind of cucumber, sprigs of mint

Glass:

Ice tea or Highball

Method:

Add the Pimm's and garnishes in an
ice-filled highball glass. Top up with
lemonade. Serve with a straw.
(See p. 6 for picture)

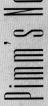

Pimm's No 1

Ingredients:

60 ml   Gin

40 ml   Lemon juice

25 ml   Sugar syrup

a dash   Angostura bitters

           Soda water

Garnish:

A slice of lemon and a cherry

Glass:

Collins

Method:

Fill the glass with cubed ice;
stir in the ingredients and top
up with soda. Garnish with a
lemon slice and cherry. Serve
with a straw.

Tom Collins

Ingredients:

150 ml   White wine
            Soda water

Garnish:

A twist of lemon peel

Glass:

Wine goblet or Highball

Method:

Put 4-5 ice cubes in the glass; pour the wine and top up with soda. Serve garnished with a twist of lemon peel.

Ingredients:

60 ml   Vodka
120 ml   Orange juice
10 ml   Galliano

Garnish:

A slice of orange and a cherry

Glass:

Highball

Method:

Pour the ingredients except the Galliano into an ice-filled highball glass. Top up with Galliano and garnish with a slice of orange and cherry. Serve with a straw.

Harvey Wallbanger

Ingredients:

30 ml	Vodka
30 ml	Blue curaçao
140 ml	Lemonade or Sprite

Garnish:

None

Glass:

Highball

Method:

Pour the vodka and blue curaçao into an ice-filled highball glass. Top up with lemonade or Sprite. Serve with a straw.

Ingredients:

60 ml	Vodka
15 ml	Peach liqueur
30 ml	Pineapple juice
10 ml	Grenadine
40 ml	Bitter lemon

Garnish:

A slice of lemon and a cherry

Glass:

Highball

Method:

Shake all the ingredients together except the bitter lemon. Strain into a highball glass and top up with bitter lemon. Add the garnish and serve..

Ingredients:

60 ml   Brandy
30 ml   Lemon juice
20 ml   Sugar syrup
            Apple juice

Garnish:

None

Glass:

Highball

Method:

Shake all the ingredients except apple juice and strain into a highball glass. Top up with apple juice.

Ingredients:

60 ml   Gin
60 ml   Orange juice
a dash   Orange curaçao

Garnish:

A twist of orange peel

Glass:

Cocktail

Method:

Shake all the ingredients together and pour into a cocktail glass. Serve garnished with a twist of orange peel.

Ingredients:

20 ml   Gin
10 ml   Cherry brandy
20 ml   Lemon juice
30 ml   Pineapple juice
a dash each of Grenadine,
Cointreau and Benedictine

Garnish:

A slice of pineapple and a cherry

Glass:

Ice tea or Highball

Method:

Shake all the ingredients together and strain into a glass. Top up with soda and garnish with a slice of pineapple and a cherry. Serve with a straw.

Ingredients:

50 ml   Woods 151 Rum
180 ml   Pineapple juice
30 ml   Lemon juice
20 ml   Apricot brandy

Garnish:

A wedge of lemon and a cherry

Glass:

Old-fashioned

Method:

Blend the first 3 ingredients together and pour into an old-fashioned glass. Add apricot brandy and serve garnished with a wedge of lemon and a cherry.

Caipirinha

Ingredients:

1	Lemon, cut into pieces
	Sugar to taste
60 ml	Cachaca or white rum

Garnish:

None

Glass:

Old-fashioned

Method:

Put the lemon in an old-fashioned glass, sprinkle with sugar. and crush together. Fill the glass with ice. Add the cachaca or white rum and serve with a stirrer.

Ingredients:

20 ml	White rum
20 ml	Dark rum
10 ml	Curaçao
10 ml	Grenadine
10 ml	Orgeat syrup
10 ml	Lemon juice

Garnish:

A wedge of lemon or pineapple and mint leaves

Glass:

Old-fashioned

Mai Tai

Method:

Fill the glass with ice cubes; pour all the ingredients, and add the garnish. Serve with a straw.

Ingredients:

1/2	Juice of lemon
30 ml	Orange juice
20 ml	Lemon juice
a dash	Grenadine
20 ml	Curaçao
20 ml	White rum
20 ml	Dark rum

Garnish:

Mint leaves

Glass:

Highball

Method:

Blend all the ingredients with crushed ice; pour into a highball glass and garnish with mint leaves. Serve with a straw.

Ingredients:

60 ml	Dark rum
30 ml	Pineapple juice
30 ml	Coconut milk
a dash	Maraschino
a dash	Orgeat syrup

Garnish:

A wedge of pineapple

Glass:

Old-fashioned

Method:

Blend all the ingredients together with 2 scoops of crushed ice and pour into an old-fashioned glass. Serve garnished with a wedge of pineapple.

Coconut Breeze

Ingredients:

60 ml	Dark rum
30 ml	Coconut cream
30 ml	Pineapple juice
a dash	Orgeat syrup

Garnish:

None

Glass:

Cocktail

Method:

Shake all the ingredients together and strain into a cocktail glass. Serve with a straw.

Ingredients:

30 ml	White rum
40 ml	Fresh orange juice
30 ml	Pineapple juice
a dash	Fresh lemon juice
10 ml	Grenadine
30 ml	Dark rum

Garnish:

A slice of pineapple and a cherry

Glass:

Highball

Method:

Shake the ingredients together except the dark rum and pour into a highball glass. Float dark rum on top and add the garnish. Serve with a straw.

Ingredients:

$1/2$	Juice of lemon
6	Mint leaves
10 ml	Sugar syrup
40 ml	Golden rum
a dash	Soda water

Garnish:

A sprig of mint

Glass:

Highball

Method:

Add lemon juice and spent shell, sugar syrup and mint leaves into the glass and muddle. Fill the glass with crushed ice. Add rum; stir until the glass frosts. Add soda water and garnish with mint. Serve with a straw.

Ingredients:

30 ml	Gin
10 ml	Cherry brandy
20 ml	Lemon juice
	Soda water

Garnish:

A slice of lemon and a cherry

Glass:

Highball or Pilsner

Method:

Fill the glass with ice cubes; shake the ingredients and strain into a highball glass. Top up with soda and garnish with a slice of lemon and a cherry. Serve with a straw.

Singapore Sling

Ingredients:

60 ml	Grapefruit juice
20 ml	Orgeat syrup
60 ml	Dark rum
120 ml	Pineapple juice

Garnish:

A wedge of pineapple

Glass:

Old-fashioned

Method:

Blend all the ingredients with crushed
ice and pour into an old-fashioned
glass. Serve garnished with a wedge
of pineapple.

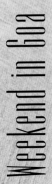

Ingredients:

60 ml	White rum
	Coke

Garnish:

A wedge of lemon

Glass:

Highball or Pilsner

Method:

Pour the rum in an ice-filled glass.
Top up with Coke; squeeze half a
lemon on top and garnish with a
wedge of lemon. Serve with a straw.

Ingredients:

30 ml	White rum
30 ml	Coconut cream
90 ml	Pineapple juice

Garnish:

A slice of pineapple and a cherry

Glass:

Champagne flute

Method:

Blend all the ingredients with a scoop of crushed ice. Pour into a champagne flute. Serve garnished with a slice of pineapple and a cherry.

Ingredients:

30 ml	Dark rum
10 ml	Brandy
30 ml	Orange juice
20 ml	Lemon juice
10 ml	Orgeat syrup

Garnish:

A slice of orange or lemon

Glass:

Old-fashioned

Method:

Blend all the ingredients with crushed ice and pour into an old-fashioned glass. Serve garnished with a slice of orange or lemon.

Ingredients:

30 ml	Gin
30 ml	Red vermouth
30 ml	Dry vermouth
30 ml	Orange juice

Garnish:

A slice of lemon and a cherry

Glass:

Cocktail

Method:

Shake all the ingredients together and strain into a cocktail glass. Serve garnished with a slice of lemon and a cherry.

Ingredients:

20 ml	Blue curaçao
40 ml	Gin
20 ml	Fresh lemon juice
a dash	Egg white

Garnish:

A twist of lemon peel

Glass:

Champagne saucer

Method:

Shake all the ingredients together and strain into a champagne saucer.

Blue Lady

Ingredients:

60 ml	Rye whisky
20 ml	Grenadine
10 ml	Orange curaçao
5 ml	Pernod

Garnish:

None

Glass:

Old-fashioned

Method:

Shake all the ingredients together and strain into an old-fashioned glass.

Ingredients:

30 ml	Apricot brandy
30 ml	Lemon juice
a dash	Angostura bitters
a dash	Orange juice

Garnish:

A slice of lemon or orange

Glass:

Wine or Sour glass

Method:

Shake all the ingredients together and strain into a wine or sour glass. Serve garnished with a slice of lemon or orange.

Apricot Sour

Ingredients:

30 ml	Orange juice
30 ml	Gin
15 ml	Campari

Garnish:

None

Glass:

Champagne flute

Method:

Shake the first 2 ingredients together and strain into a champagne flute. Add campari on top.

Ingredients:

60 ml	Desired spirit
30 ml	Lemon juice
10 ml	Grenadine
	Soda water (optional)

Garnish:

A mint sprig and a slice of lemon

Glass:

Wine goblet

Method:

Shake all the ingredients together except the soda water. Add soda water only if desired. Serve garnished with a mint sprig and lemon slice.

Daisy

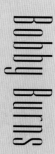

Ingredients:

50 ml	Scotch
30 ml	Sweet vermouth
3 dashes	Benedictine

Garnish:

A twisted lemon peel .

Glass:

Old-fashioned

Method:

Pour the ingredients into an ice-filled old-fashioned glass and stir well. Serve garnished with a twisted lemon peel.

Martini-American Style

Ingredients:

60 ml	Gin or Vodka
2 drops	Dry vermouth

Garnish:

An olive or twisted lemon peel

Glass:

Martini

Method:

Stir all the ingredients together and strain or if served on the rocks, it should be built in rock glass. Add the garnish and serve.

Ingredients:

30 ml	Bourbon
10 ml	Strega
10 ml	Anisette

Garnish:

A twisted orange peel

Glass:

Cocktail

Method:

Stir all the ingredients together and strain into a cocktail glass. Serve garnished with a twisted orange peel.

Ingredients:

60 ml	Bourbon
30 ml	Dry vermouth
30 ml	Orange curaçao
a dash	Grenadine

Garnish:

Cocktail cherry and an orange slice

Glass:

Old-fashioned

Method:

Pour all the ingredients into an ice-filled old-fashioned glass and stir well. Serve garnished with a cocktail cherry and an orange slice.

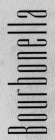

Ingredients:

60 ml	Scotch
30 ml	Fresh lemon juice
25 ml	Gomme syrup
a dash	Egg white
a dash	Angostura bitters

Garnish:

A slice of lemon and a cherry

Glass:

Cocktail or Sour glass

Method:

Shake all the ingredients together. Strain into a double cocktail glass or a special sour glass. Serve garnished with a slice of lemon and a cherry.

Whisky Sour

Ingredients:

30 ml	Brandy
10 ml	Cherry brandy
30 ml	Lemon juice

Garnish:

A slice of lemon or orange and a cocktail cherry

Glass:

Wine goblet

Method:

Fill the goblet with crushed ice and build the drink. Serve garnished with a slice of lemon or orange and a cherry.

Ingredients:

1	Sugar cube
3 drops	Angostura bitters
60 ml	Bourbon
	Soda water / Ginger-ale

Garnish:

A slice of orange and a cherry

Glass:

Old-fashioned

Method:

Soak the sugar cube in angostura bitters and drop into an old-fashioned glass. Add bourbon and powder the sugar cube. Fill the glass with ice; add the garnish and top up with soda or ginger-ale.

Ingredients:

30 ml	Tequila
15 ml	Galliano
15 ml	Crème de banane
15 ml	Cream
a dash	Grenadine
a dash	Lemon juice

Garnish:

None

Glass:

Champagne saucer

Method:

Shake all the ingredients; strain into a champagne saucer and stir well.

Sunrise

Ingredients:

30 ml	Vodka
30 ml	Cointreau
30 ml	Lemon juice

Garnish:

A cocktail cherry

Glass:

Cocktail

Method

Shake all the ingredients together and strain into a cocktail glass.

Ingredients:

60 ml	Gin
30 ml	Lime juice cordial
	Soda water (optional)

Garnish:

A wedge of lemon

Glass:

Old-fashioned

Method:

Pour all the ingredients into an old-fashioned glass except soda water. Stir well. Serve on the rocks, with a splash of soda water, if desired. Garnish with a wedge of lemon.

Ingredients:

60 ml	Brandy
20 ml	Orange curaçao
20 ml	Pineapple juice
a dash	Angostura bitters

Garnish:

A twisted lemon peel and a cherry

Glass:

Cocktail

Method:

Shake all the ingredients together and pour into a cocktail glass. Serve garnished with a twisted lemon peel and a cherry.

Ingredients:

40 ml	Tequila
40 ml	Lemon juice
20 ml	Orange curaçao

Garnish:

Rim the glass with salt

Glass:

Cocktail

Margarita

Method:

Shake all the ingredients together and strain into a cocktail glass.

Ingredients:

45 ml	Rye whisky
20 ml	Red vermouth
a dash	Angostura bitters

Garnish:

A cherry

Glass:

Cocktail

Method:

Stir all the ingredients together and strain into a cocktail glass or if served on the rocks, it should be built in rock glass. Serve garnished with a cherry.

Ingredients:

45 ml	Blended Irish whiskey
20 ml	Lemon juice
15 ml	Sugar syrup
a dash	Orange juice
a dash	Angostura bitters

Garnish:

A slice of orange and a cherry

Glass:

Wine or Sour glass

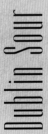

Dublin Sour

Method:

Shake all the ingredients together and strain into the glass.

Ingredients:

60 ml	Vodka
15 ml	Cointreau
20 ml	Cranberry juice

Garnish:

A twisted orange peel

Glass:

Cocktail

Method:

Shake all the ingredients and strain into a cocktail glass. Serve garnished with a twisted orange peel.

Ingredients:

50 ml	Gin
25 ml	Lemon juice
25 ml	Cointreau
a dash	Egg white

Garnish:

A cocktail cherry

Glass:

Cocktail

Method:

Shake all the ingredients together and strain into a cocktail glass.

White Lady

Ingredients:

45 ml	Vodka
20 ml	Lemon juice
15 ml	Sugar syrup
$1/2$	Banana, small

Garnish:

None

Glass:

Cocktail

Method:

Blend all the ingredients with the crushed ice and pour into a cocktail glass. Serve with a straw.

Ingredients:

30 ml	Gin
30 ml	Sweet vermouth
30 ml	Campari
	Soda water (optional)

Garnish:

A slice of orange

Glass:

Highball

Method:

Build the drink in an ice-filled highball glass. Garnish with a slice of orange. Serve with a stirrer.

Negroni

Ingredients:

40 ml	Gin
20 ml	Apricot brandy
20 ml	Orange juice

Garnish:

A slice of lemon and a cherry

Glass:

Old-fashioned

Method:

Shake all the ingredients together and strain into an old-fashioned glass. Serve garnished with a slice of lemon and a cherry.

Ingredients:

60 ml	Scotch
30 ml	Sweet vermouth
a dash	Angostura bitters

Garnish:

A cocktail cherry

Glass:

Champagne saucer

Method:

Pour all the ingredients into a champagne saucer and stir well. Serve garnished with a cherry.

Ingredients:

60 ml	Vodka
15 ml	Crème de cassis

Garnish:

None

Glass:

Cocktail

Method:

Stir vodka and crème de cassis and strain into a cocktail glass.

Black Russian

Ingredients:

30 ml	Vodka
30 ml	Kahlua

Garnish:

None

Glass:

Old-fashioned

Method:

Build the drink in an ice-filled old-fashioned glass.

Ingredients:

30 ml   Kahlua
30 ml   Crème de menthe
            (white)
40 ml   High fat content cream

Garnish:

None

Glass:

Cocktail

Method:

Shake all the ingredients gently and pour into a cocktail glass.

Coffee Grasshopper

Ingredients

30 ml   Crème de cacao
            (white)
30 ml   Crème de menthe
            (green)
30 ml   Cream

Garnish:

None

Glass:

Champagne saucer

Method:

Shake the ingredients gently and strain into a champagne saucer.

Grasshopper

Ingredients:

30 ml	Galliano
30 ml	Crème de cacao (white)
30 ml	High fat content cream

Garnish:

None

Glass:

Champagne saucer

Method:

Shake all the ingredients gently and pour into a champagne saucer.

Ingredients:

2 barspoons	Demerara sugar
60 ml	Irish whiskey
200 ml	Hot black coffee
40 ml	Baileys Irish cream

Garnish:

None

Glass:

Irish coffee

Method:

Add the sugar and whiskey into the glass containing hot black coffee. Stir until the sugar dissolves completely. Then float the Baileys over the back of a barspoon. (See p. 13 for picture)

Ingredients:

30 ml   Brandy

30 ml   Benedictine

Garnish:

None

Glass:

Brandy snifter

Method:

Pour the ingredients into a brandy snifter and serve warm. Can also be served on the rocks.

Ingredients:

30 ml   Kahlua

30 ml   Baileys Irish cream

30 ml   Cointreau

Garnish:

None

Glass:

Shooter

Method:

Layer the ingredients in a shooter glass in the above order using the back of a spoon .

Ingredients:

50 ml   Kahlua

25 ml   High fat content cream

$^1/_2$ Pulped banana, small

Garnish:

None

Glass:

Champagne saucer

Method:

Shake all the ingredients gently and pour into a champagne saucer.

Ingredients:

30 ml   Galliano

30 ml   Cointreau

30 ml   Orange juice

30 ml   Cream

Garnish:

None

Glass:

Cocktail

Method:

Shake all the ingredients gently and strain into a cocktail glass.

Ingredients:

10 ml	Crème de cacao
10 ml	Crème de violette
10 ml	Yellow chartreuse
10 ml	Maraschino
10 ml	Benedictine
10 ml	Brandy

Garnish:

None

Glass:

Shooter

Method:

Build the drink in a shooter glass using the back of a teaspoon taking care to keep the ingredients separate.

Ingredients:

40 ml	Tequila
40 ml	Crème de cacao (white)
40 ml	Cream
10 ml	Grenadine

Garnish:

A cocktail cherry

Glass:

Cocktail

Method:

Blend all the ingredients together with a scoop of crushed ice. Pour into a cocktail glass and garnish with a cocktail cherry.

Silk Stocking

Pink Flamingo

Ingredients:

60 ml	Amaretto
4	Pulped strawberries
40 ml	Cream

Garnish:

None

Glass:

Cocktail

Method:

Shake all the ingredients gently and strain into a cocktail glass.

Godfather

Ingredients:

60 ml	Scotch or bourbon
30 ml	Amaretto

Garnish:

None

Glass:

Old-fashioned

Method:

Build the drink into an ice-filled old-fashioned glass..

Ingredients:

30 ml   Brandy
30 ml   Crème de cacao
40 ml   High fat content cream

Garnish:

Grated nutmeg

Glass:

Brandy snifter

Method:

Shake all the ingredients gently and pour into a brandy snifter. Serve sprinkled with nutmeg.

Ingredients:

30 ml   Tequila
30 ml   Kahlua

Garnish:

None

Glass:

Old-fashioned

Method:

Build the drink in an ice-filled old-fashioned glass.

Brave Bull

Ingredients:

570 ml	Water
225 gm	Granulated sugar
1	Cinnamon stick
4	Cloves
2	Lemons, sliced
1 bottle	Burgundy
Honey to taste	

Garnish:

Lemon slice studded with cloves

Glass:

Wine goblet

Method:

Boil the water with the sugar, cinnamon and cloves for 5 minutes. Add the lemons and allow to stand for 10 minutes. Add burgundy and heat slowly but do not allow to boil. Serve very hot. (Makes: 8-10 glasses)

Ingredients:

1 bottle	Dark rum
250 ml	Honey
400 ml	Lemon juice
4	Cinnamon sticks
20	Cloves
Demerara sugar to taste	

Garnish:

A slice of lemon

Glass:

Wine goblet

Method:

Dissolve honey in 1 cup boiling water. Add half lemon juice and all the rum. Adjust the taste by adding more lemon juice or sugar. Grind cinnamon and cloves, tie in a muslin cloth and drop into the mixture. Leave for 12 hours, remove muslin, add 2 lt water and bring to the boil an hour before serving. (Makes: 15 glasses)

Mistletoe Mull

Ingredients:

2 dozens	Strawberries
2 slices	Pineapples, chopped
2 tbsp	Caster sugar
60 ml	Water
60 ml	Maraschino
1 bottle	Dry sparkling wine
	Soda water

Garnish:
A slice of pineapple

Glass:
Wine goblet

Method:
Blend fruits, sugar, and water into a purée. Pour into an ice-filled jug. Add remaining ingredients and stir well.

Ingredients:

60 ml	Tequila
180 ml	Orange juice
20 ml	Grenadine

Garnish:
A slice of orange and a cocktail cherry

Glass:
Ice tea or Highball

Method:
Half fill the glass with ice and pour tequila, orange juice, and then grenadine so that it sinks to the bottom.

Ingredients :

2 bottles	Red wine
1 lt	Soda or lemonade
150 ml	Brandy (grape or any fruit)
1 cup	Granulated sugar
300 ml	Fresh orange juice
200 ml	Lemon juice

Garnish:

Sliced oranges, lemons, peaches, strawberries or mangoes.

Glass:

Wine goblet

Method:

Pour half of each ingredient into a large container. Stir until the sugar dissolves completely. Taste and adjust proportions accordingly. Store in a cool place for about 6 hours; add the garnish and ice just before serving. Serve with a straw.

Ingredients:

2 bottles	Claret
85 gm	Sugar
140 ml	Water
2	Juice of oranges
2	Juice of lemons
1 lt	Soda water

Garnish:

A slice and rind each of an orange and lemon

Glass:

Wine goblet

Method:

Stir all the ingredients together until the sugar dissolves completely. Refrigerate until ready to serve. Add soda and serve garnished with a slice and rind each of an orange and lemon. (Makes: 14-16 glasses)

Claret Cup

Ingredients:

60 ml   Vodka
90 ml   Grapefruit juice
90 ml   Cranberry juice

Garnish:

A wedge of grapefruit

Glass:

Highball

Method:

Build the drink in a highball glass half-filled with ice. Serve garnished with a wedge of grapefruit.

Ingredients:

60 ml   Vodka
30 ml   Sweet lime juice
120 ml   Ginger-ale

Garnish:

A lemon wedge and sprig of mint

Glass:

Highball

Method:

Pour all the ingredients except ginger-ale into an ice-filled highball glass. Stir in the ginger-ale. Garnish with a lemon wedge and mint sprig. Serve with a straw.

Monsoon Mule

Ingredients:

180 ml   Tomato juice

20 ml   Lemon juice

2 dashes   Worcestershire sauce

Celery salt to taste

Garnish:

A celery stick

Glass:

Wine goblet or Highball

Method:

Shake all the ingredients together.
Strain into a wine goblet or an
ice-filled highball glass. Serve
garnished with a celery stick.

Virgin Mary

Ingredients:

250 ml   Ginger-ale

25 ml   Grenadine

Garnish:

A slice of lemon and a cherry

Glass:

Highball

Method:

Build the drink in a highball glass
half-filled with ice. Serve garnished
with a slice of lemon and a cherry.

Ingredients:

50 ml	Orange juice
50 ml	Lemon juice
50 ml	Lime juice cordial
2 dashes	Grenadine
1	Egg yolk

Garnish:

A slice of orange and a cherry

Glass:

Cocktail

Method:

Shake all the ingredients and strain into a cocktail glass half-filled with ice.

Ingredients:

1 dozen	Mint sprigs
1 cup	Boiling water
1.2 lt	Cold water
Granulated sugar to taste	

Garnish:

Lemon peel and mint sprigs

Glass:

Ice tea

Method:

Steep mint and boiling water in a pot for at least 30 minutes. Strain and allow to cool. Combine with cold water in a large jug. Add sugar and stir until dissolved. Serve with ice and garnish with lemon peel and mint sprigs.

Iced Fresh Mint Tea

Ingredients:

100 gm	Banana, chopped
4	Strawberries, chopped
100 gm	Pineapple, chopped
50 ml	Mango juice

Garnish:

Pineapple slice and a strawberry

Glass:

Highball or Small pilsner

Method:

Blend all the ingredients with a scoop of crushed ice. Pour into a highball or small pilsner glass. Garnish and serve with a straw.

Ingredients :

2 scoops	Lemon sorbet
1	Banana
60 ml	Pineapple juice

Garnish:

None

Glass:

Ice tea or Highball

Method:

Blend all the ingredients, pour into a glass and serve with a straw.

Ingredients:

80 ml	Lemon juice
80 ml	Orange juice
80 ml	Pineapple juice
20 ml	Sugar syrup

Garnish:

A slice of orange and a cocktail cherry

Glass:

Highball

Method:

Shake all the ingredients together and strain into a highball glass containing 3-4 cubes of ice. Serve garnished with

Ingredients:

60 ml	Coconut cream (sweet)
150 ml	Pineapple juice

Garnish:

A wedge of pineapple and a cocktail cherry

Glass:

Champagne flute

Method:

Blend all the ingredients and pour into a highball glass. Garnish with a pineapple wedge and a cherry. Serve with a straw.

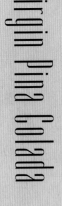

Index

Rum

Bombay High 40
Caipirinha 38
Coconut Breeze 39
Cuba Libra 43
Frozen Daiquiri 27
Mai Tai 38
Mojito 42
Pina Colada 44
Planter's Punch 40
Scorpion 44
Toddy 80
Weekend in Goa 43
Zombie 39
151 + ... 37

Tequila

Brave Bull 78
Freddy Fudpucker 20
Margarita 60
Sunrise 57
Silk Stocking 76
Tequila Sunrise 82

Vodka

Balalaika 58
Black Russian 68
Bloody Caesar & Family 23
Bloody Mary 22
Blue Lagoon 33
Cosmopolitan 62
Freddy Fudpucker 20

Fuzzy Screwdriver 22
Harvey Wallbanger 30
Lucky Dogra 65
Martini–American Style 52
Midnight Mood 68
Monsoon Mule 86
Sea Breeze 86
Screwdriver 24
Virginia 33

Whisky

Bobby Burns 52
Bourbonella 53
Dublin Coffee 71
Dublin Sour 61
Godfather 77
Kentucky Sunset 53
Manhattan 61
Millionaire 49
Mint Julep 28
Old Fashioned 57
Whisky Sour 54
Rob Roy 66

Wine

Claret Cup 85
Kir 17
Mistletoe Mull 80
Peace Cup 82
Sangria 85
Spritzer 30